STŌRIES of SHE

Lucy Adams

Book Leaf
Publishing

India | USA | UK

Presentation by *BookLeaf Publishing*

Web: www.bookleafpub.com

E-mail: info@bookleafpub.com

ISBN: 9789358738162

First edition 2023

To all Guardians of the Divine light,

Shine bright

ACKNOWLEDGEMENT

An ode to the Goddess

PREFACE

May these words melt into your heart, to bring you healing and empowerment as you feel called to receive it. Blessings to all that read them.

01 Your gifts - an invitation to the Goddess

I see you

Writhing with something so much bigger than
yourself
Trying so desperately to understand and make
sense of emotions that no words can express
I see the frustration
The tears pouring down your cheeks
As you search for the logic and reasonAn
answer to make it stop
You are look for healing, redemption, someone
who can fix it for you

Stop my love
Let go of your need to know

You are here
On the precipice of a great change
Where the Goddess is asking you to take her
side and become a messenger of her light
Stop trying to rid yourself of the confusion
And surrender into what it's here to teach you
How it is allowing you to grow
This is a shift in your entire consciousness

The world as you know it

She is moving through you
A wave you cannot describe
She is a felt sense
A cleansing
A deep re-birth that often feels like insanity to
the uninitiated

But you are safe
And you have broken open to receive
So sit in silence to listen
Create stillness to invoke calm
& soften your body to become a channel for her
light to move through

Her path is not easy - it's redemption and
correction of thousands of years of wrongdoing
Yet you are not lost
If you are here it was already your choice
If you are here you already carry all that you
need
If you are here your soul was planted on earth as
a sacred priestess of the old ways
Your gifts are needed now
Only you can serve this role

Step into the invitation
Say yes when you are ready

Become the student
And she will teach you
She will show you all there is to know
To remember
She will reconnect you to your divine purpose
on this earth
The initiation to the Goddess

Your yes is sacred and only yours to give
You will know when
Allow don't force

AHO sisters
As one we all rise.

02 Whispers of the womb - long forgotten truths

Deep in the body of the Feminine
The womb of truth
Whispering to you
Listen to hear
Listen to know
Listen to receive
She is guiding you
She holds your truth
She knows your divine path
The way to walk on this journey through life
A mystic priestess
A wise woman
A safe space to feel
She holds it all
Deep in the body of the Feminine
She will birth your light
Your creations into the world
She will birth your pains
Releasing your fears and old-truths
On her monthly cycle she renews and forgives
Offers you the chance to adjust the life you live
Tune in and listen to her secrets
Her stories
The memories she holds

Ask for her medicine, her message, her magick
Let her become your muse
Place both hands on your womb and ask for her
love
Her divine guidance
She will always lead you home
Back to your Self
Back to your truth
Back to your body
This Earthside portal to the Divine realms
Your primal knowing
Your nous wisdom
Comes through your womb
Let her voice speak to you
Listen to hear
Listen to know
Listen to receive
She is guiding you
She holds your truth.

03 Your unique expression - the world needs your light

Stop apologising for who you are
The world needs you in your true form
Your most authentic nature expressed through
your thoughts, words, and desires
Your creations deserve to be fuelled by Your
passions
Your pains and your unique story
It's yours to tell
No one else's
We have all been so conditioned to adapt
To fit it
To conform
Seeking validation outside of ourselves
And rejecting the whispers of truth that reside
within
You do a disservice to yourself when you choose
to live this way
The world needs you and your magic
Your unique gifts
Your unique insights
When each of us chooses to take radical
responsibility for the light we've each been
gifted
A pattern emerges

One where we each learn from the other
We each hold a small part of the nights sky
And together birth the cosmos
You are your own star
Don't try to imitate someone else's
We don't need two of the same
We need you as you were born to be
The essence you were birthed to bring here, now
Be inspired and motivated and encouraged by
the way others shine
But hone that focus back into your heart
And tune into your own light
The way through the darkness comes when the
whole path is lit
Be brave enough to step beyond what you know
of life
To the part where you bring colour
Depth
Humility
Wisdom
Joy
Play
Life.

04 Jupiter's expansion - you are worthy

Fizzing in my cells
A long forgotten story
I am connected
We are all one
My vision is clearer
My heart full
Bursting with ideas
Bursting with love
An overflowing tidal wave of emotions pours
through me
Washing away the doubt and fear
Fireworks of joy explode in my sacral
Life-force energy bursting through my human
seams
I sit in quiet contemplation
Opening to receive this divine white channel of
light
It pours through my crown
Encasing me in a shield of hope
Dousing me in a rush of ecstasy
Electricity
Forgiveness
Acceptance
The mind is silenced

The body stilled
My infinite potential presented to me
"I know this"
It's so familiar
As though it never left my side
When was it taken
This deep sense of my own worth
Who stole it from me
When did I forget
Become separate from the other
Isolated in my own insanity
As my aura expands and connects the dots
A smile creeps on my face
Hidden in the shadows is the knowing
That all along it resided within me
Tethered between doubt and resolution
Belief pulled up to the surface
I will nurture you
I will keep you afloat
Throw you up into the skies where I can watch
you shine at night
Through the darkness of life
My lucky star
My hope
My joy
Knowing that the clouds may sometimes cloak
your light
But you are never lost.

05 The Lions Gate - wish upon a star

It's okay to let things crumble, to take a break
from being strong, to claim your vulnerability
and the times that you've been wrong.

Let it go with a blessing - that to be humbled is a
gift.
That from this fresh perspective you have gained
a brand new wish.

But don't rush to climb the mountain - don't just
focus on it's peak.
See the valleys, streams, and ocean breeze that
carry your weary feet.

Notice all the things that guide you, the
moments that build to where you'll be.
Don't forget the journey along the way, or miss
the signs you wished to see.

Use your breath to reach your heartspace.
Every day drop in to feel.

Because to manifest is not a made up feat, it's
your destiny revealed.

And when you stop to listen,

Dial in but don't interfere,
You will receive a message - one you didn't
know was yours to hear.

At first it might sound strange
Or too big for who you are.

That's only because you've forgotten,
That your very soul was birthed from stars.

As Sirius shines brightly
Bringing the heavens to your door

Open your heart a little wider - journey inwards
to explore.
This gift of light that you are granted

From your cosmic guides above
As you feel yourself break open

Trust you are held firmly in their love.

06 The prayer of Persephone - flowers from the underworld

Something is growing beneath the darkness
A wave of mystery yet to be understood
The dark goddess howling at the moon
Her pain too great for humanity
Destruction pulling at the hearts of all on earth
As we abandon our mother and ourselves

Yet I trust in what's coming
That our sacrifices are for a greater good
It's so hard to be in it
To carry these burdens
And watch the world burn
My heart is too fragile and I feel
helplessly alone
Out of my depth
Lost & scared
But so aware of what's moving
Birthing
Lurking in the shadows waiting for renewal

The difference between a choice and a calling is
throwing your heart and soul behind a feeling
without the logic to understand why
I do not know why
or how
or when
So please don't ask me

Hold my hand and let's walk together
Trust that the madness will find resolution
Share stories of what feels like our truth
Learn to love again in ways that connect us
That light a path for the new way thats upon us
The new wave for humanity
The one that will grow from the ashes of what
we have destroyed
That will blossom into flowers for a new
generation of man to enjoy

The seeds of our hope will become the fruit of
the future
The gardens will grow when we fertilise the soil
Our journey through the underworld is only half
of the cycle
The re-birth is on the other side.

07 A journey through grief - Chiron's path

Peace & love
A healing balm
Surrounded by white light
Held
Supported
Loved
Internal flame burning bright
Whispering your name
Protection
Spirit
Guidance
You are not alone
You are met on your path by all those that
walked before you
Ancestors
Goddesses
Your angels surround you
Safety
Strength
Comfort in your suffering
Walk it out
Push through
This is not the end
This is not forever

The opening of a portal
The closing of an expired truth
Grief is the tunnel through despair
That leads you on to a higher expression of
yourself
A developed consciousness
Deepened empathy
Nothing is the same yet all the mundane things
carry on
A time warp
Loneliness
You barely recognise yourself in mourning
Drop inwards
You are there
Bring that light through
You will shine
Not right now
Don't force
There's no need
But soon
One day
This will become part of your story
The one you came to live
Your pain will become your growth
Your wounds your wings
You will be the peace & love
The healing balm for others in their own journey
through grief.

08 Release - it's safe to let go

My love I want you to close your eyes
Take a deep breath inwards
And feel your heart as she beats in your chest
Feel the waves of emotion as they come
crashing down
Set them free
Wade deep
I promise you you won't drown
Hold my hand if you need touch
Start by dipping your toes in the depth of your
soul
Feel yourself slipping away
You are safe in your own reality
Allow yourself to slow and feel
The dark may scare you
But learning to love yourself without the light of
another is what will free you
You can let go now
You can feel the way towards the sound of your
soul as she calls
Don't be afraid
Trust in her release.

09 The power of a PAUSE - connecting to Self

You told me to stop
To pause
To wonder
And at first I couldn't understand why
I'd fidget
And fumble
My thoughts would get lost
Caught up in the gossip
And the time it would cost me
To soften my grip
And loosen my mind
To take a deep breath into the earth
And exhale to the sky
I felt a connection
It strengthened until
Suddenly I found myself craving the still
Beyond that time portal
Nothing was lost
Everything gained
There wasn't a cost
It was liberating
Freeing
Revealing and pure
My true sense of self

Found asking for more
But more of nothing
And a substance to something
It didn't make sense
And that's why I loved it
To open my heart
Simply to receive
No agenda
No motive
Returning to peace.

10 Evolution - The change we all seek to find

The beauty of life
The mystery
The secret
The subtle knowing
The felt sense

It all starts and ends with you
With your thoughts
Your chosen expressions
Your reactions
Your responses
Your choices

With your courage to delve within

How far will you open
How much will you remain closed

These are the markers of how fully you will live
How deeply you will experience life
To be truly expansive you cannot let fear contain
you
You must allow love to break you wide open
Open to receive

To let life in

Let it shape you
Mould and re-mould you over and over
Give yourself permission to grow
and change
and form new perspectives
To stay stuck in one version of your Self, is to
limit your experience

Be curious
Playful
Daring

Find your own truth
And challenge it regularly

The end goal is not to have all the answers
It's to have asked all the questions your heart is
burning to know
So start exploring

And never stop.

11 Re-birthing - honouring sacred rest

I felt the strength coming up
Breaking back through
I knew she would
I knew she was there
I left her to rest
To delve deeper
To really uncover the source of what was
holding me back
To find the vulnerability and cradle it
Refill it with love
Tell that part of my soul that she was okay
That I could feel through the pain
Honour it and let it go
Sometimes being strong is exhausting and
actually relenting to pain is necessary
I needed to take time to feel sad in order to work
through my grief
And because of that I feel so much stronger
It's not worth smiling through the pain
Pretending you're okay when you're hurting
Don't be afraid to take the time to address it
Face your fears head on
What are they trying to tell you?
I promise that you are stronger than you feel

Tougher than you think
That there's a power and a fire within you that
needs you to light it
Sometimes we need to sit in darkness to notice
the tiny embers re-emerge
Nurture those sparks
The flames of renaissance.

12 Touch - ignite with your senses

In a world driven mad by the confines of the
mind
I invite you to return to the pulse of mankind.

The body you live in
That houses your soul
Is more than the number of years you are old.

She birthed with the sun and the moon in the sky
But carries the codes of all loved ones passed by
Deep inside your own DNA
They still whisper, and shape you
Listen to what they say.

We all have 5 senses to feel what we know
Deep down in our bodies
The truths of long ago.

And it's our duty to listen
With optimum care
To the journey's and lessons
Of before we came here.

Past lives carry value

But so does the now
Your invite to slow down and connect with the
ground.

Tune into your womb, your heart and third eye
Allow them to unlock all the codes that reside.

13 Friday the thirteenth - reclaim this sacred blessing

Thirteen
The sacred number
13 moons
13 bleeds
Our cycles were forgotten - lost and shamed
Along with our many needs

We have been made to fear their power
Taught to live within their loss
Let's call them back. Welcome them in
Tune into our lost cycles
And connect with what it's cost.

This is Mother Earth syncing with your womb
Ready to birth creation through you
New life and ideas gifted
For you to blossom and to bloom.

Be the vessel
Become the chalice
Know your sacred worth
Just as old thoughts and stories wait to purge
The cycles of release and rebirth.

To be of service to the whole
Man, woman, & child
To reclaim this sacred blessing
We need you pure, primal, and wild.

Friday - Venus day
Our pleasure & desires known
Connected to our innermost feelings
and senses abandoned long ago.

Claim them back
Welcome them back
Drop into that space
What's blocking you
Preventing you
From living life at your own pace?

Authentically expressing
Sounding out your truth
Let it out - scream it out
Unleash the madness within you.

Purging and returning
Cleansing and reviving
You have not gone mad
You are not possessed
You are ridding yourself of the external stress.

Purifying your sacred vessel

Of its toxic unrest
Sick with poison
Full of rage
Of the lies they sent to test you
And to tame.

You are not mad you are feeling
And feelings are wrong they say
Because with feeling you will not be controlled
You will carve out your own way

You are coming to your senses
Unravelling at the seams
You look mad when you refuse to conform
Your inner beauty demanding to be seen.

Friday the thirteenth
The call from Goddess
An invitation to walk her path
Held by her powerful embrace
As you connect to your ancient past.

Be empowered by the Goddess
Drawn through the human realms to receive
encoded secrets,
Connected to the veils beyond
For all courageous enough to seek them.

Open to receive from the divine

Unlock - awake - let her in
Sit with her
Pray to her
Let the dance with her begin.

Celebrate and cherish her
Find the spark in your own heart
Nurture it
Sink into your body
Reclaim every single part.

Release all the heavy burdens
That were never really yours
This day want's to set you free
To steer you back on course.

That's why they stole it from us
Take it back
Reclaim this sacred blessing

A kiss from the Goddess.
Shrouding you in her divine light
A natural, deeply loved undressing.

A washing of your sins
A return to your true worth
A blessing to root your embodied Self
Back firmly on this Earth.

14 Returning to Lilith - abandon your perfection

I heard her name and curiosity spoke to me
Tuned in to her spirit and instantly woke to thee
I felt her memory stir awake my past lives
I had no doubt my soul returned to fight for her
flight.

Not just hers, but the stand that she took for all
women
When she stood up to Adam, committing our
original sin.
Demanding our equality, and refusing to submit,
Banished from the garden because man could
not admit,
That women have a place beside not just
beneath,
It gave us too much power,
So they banished her completely.
Replaced with lovely Eve, the sweet maiden of
mans rib.
Yet Lilith whispered in her ear,
And into the apple of humanity she bit.

Sin one and sin us all.
Don't you see we're all connected

Stop using power to control
What should be universally respected.

When Lilith flew from the garden, the truth of
the world could begin
Where we will all flirt with temptation and are
burdened by our sins.
Ego came second, her courage came first
On her beautiful wings she chose to carry the
curse.
That women must choose, to be strong or obey
To be the temptress the predator
Or the good girl and prey.
She asks us to look between the guise of the veil
To notice that life exists between the heaven and
the hell.

She needs not our recognition
She's content on her own
She's laughing and joking
And poking fun at your soul.
"Stop hiding the parts of yourself you don't
think life will accept
On your deathbed conformity is the very thing
you'll regret.
When you could have expressed that light you
keep small,
Why not follow your heart, unsubscribe from it
all."

15 Saturn's Return - realigning your true path

So let me tell you what's changed.
You've shed layers you never even knew you had
You stretched into space you never even knew existed
You cried tears you never thought you'd be strong enough to let go of
You accepted parts of yourself you never believed you could truly love
You grew into the sort of women you have always admired
You took on a new role
One that fits so beautifully with your soul
You discovered a purpose that has made your heart feel so full that tears of happiness have become your new normal
You realised that at some point you started to breathe again
You began to tell your story
You found ways and words to communicate how you truly feel, both internally and externally and you found freedom through those expressions
You let go of an old version of you

One that served you so well and protected you
through some really tough times
You blessed that part of yourself and you were
kind
You were understanding and that's when you
understood
You stood strongly beside your most vulnerable
self and quietly said it's okay to both
You recognised the power growing in your belly
to be more, do more, and let go
To just surrender into your being, into the arms
of this crazy journey we call life
You gave up some of the things that were always
holding you back, tying you up
You cut back those restrictions
And you built a new path
One you happily skip down barefoot
One paved with sand warmed by the sun
You followed your heart and let your intuition
guide the way
You took your time
You are taking your time
And you are being rewarded with the true
feeling of presence
For the first time you feel at home
In your skin
In the fabulous temple of your own body, mind,
spirit and soul
Sister you are all of this

All of this is within you
The work you have done is simply the beginning
From my heart to yours keep following your
inner voice
She was coaxed from her shell for the world to
hear her roar
You never have to be small again
Continue to grow my love
Continue to stretch your love out into the
universe
You are radiant
What's changed is that you finally recognise it is
so.

16 Ever-changing
- permission to grow

Live your life without a point to prove
Tune into your desires and your pains
Express both
Neglect neither
Embrace the whole vision of who you are.

Care not for the validation of others
Stay open to learning from the opinions that
matter to you
Move away from the ones that don't
You can't hold it all
It will cloud your insights
And take away your truth.

Learn to ignite your own flames
Your creativity
Your thought-streams
Your feelings
Learn to move in the direction of your dreams
Beyond every challenge that will arise.

Be the master of your energy
Motivate and discipline your goals
Flow in a way that moves with life

Your rhythm
Your muse.

Distractions and challenge will come along
Always
And it's upto you to stay strong
Focused
Determined
In your lane
Steadfast in your truth and desires.

So know them
Own them
Build that stable familiarity and check in
regularly
Because you merge and evolve constantly
Ever changing
Never the same as yesterday.

Embrace that
Let that be a fact
Permission to grow
What a gift.

17 Lightworker - A call out from the Goddess

There will always be external voices.
When you choose different
You challenge their same
They will always belittle your wider known
dreams
'cause your maybe, it threatens their safe.
Believing in unknown realms
Is rejecting their truth
Not everyone feels ready to unearth their roots
That sacred stability that tells us not to move.

We've all been fed lies
And told not to think
We've been told how to dance
What to eat
When to drink
Forgotten to breathe
To connect to our wombs
Both in women
Our mothers
And the earth that holds you.

It's equally true
That not all will go first

We won't rush to the fire when we know we'll
get burnt
To feel the flames tear open hearts and lap at
your soul
To step through the portal into the dark and
unknown.
That's how you know you've been chosen by
Her
Goddess
Protectress
Sacred warrior
It's not about right or wrong
or better or worse
but belonging and longing and wanting more
than this curse.

To feel shut off
And vacant
Disconnected
And lost
She's here to remind you the true human cost
Of ignoring your heart song
Forgetting the call
For better or worse you're here to embrace it all.
Something is amiss
and always has been
Your search for your truth
Your light to be seen
You're not here to threaten my love

That I know
But not everyone is ready
I hear you
Now go.
Step into the light
Find your torch
Light your flame
Remember your story
Take hold of your name
Write the truth in the sand
Touch the earth with your palms
With the love of the Goddess you will come to
no harm.

Through the darkness of winter
Allow seeds to sink
Down into the soil
And allow them to drink
From the well of creation
The earth mothers milk
Nurtured protected and held in the still.
For when Spring returns
You too will bloom out
You will blossom and grow
Beyond all reasonable doubt.

18 A New Earth - coming together

A prayer for this Earth
A song to be sung
Unravelling
Shining
United as one
We all became separate
It fractured our souls
A truth and a mystery everyone knows
Deep down in our core we don't want this alone
We want intimacy, friendship, a lover and home
So why are we fighting, competing, comparing
When we could be supporting and healing and
sharing
I often wonder when the seed was planted
This nemesis rooted
Our innocence doubted
And now we're all cursed to fear our own kin
We abandon our love
Focus mostly on sin
It's fear that contains us
That keeps us all trapped
Holding us hostage and doubting the facts
Neglecting our primal love for the whole
Rejecting our tribal nature

Leading to our fall
Love and stability
Safety and calm
Those are the true values that keep us from harm
We must lower our weapons of power and greed
And return to the heart
We must all plant a seed
To grow a new earth for the children to come
Nurture the progress that's already begun
To change the way we all act and think
And invite in a new way
A new truth to drink
When brothers and sisters unite as one kin
A new wave of love - let's welcome it in.

19 Angel of the Divine - born to be whole

You are an angel of the divine
A bright light that shines through the darkness
Your heart expansive and full
Despite the burdens you have carried
You stand tall
Undefined by the words cast from your past
Carved into fresh rock
You are the simple essence of you
Complete with your shadow
You are an army
A river
A swarm of bees
Ready. Strong. poised.
You may be feared for your power
Your ability to kill, attack, defy
But don't let this define you
Your need to protect, your ability to love
There is a need for you, and your rage
A place for your passion and lust
Don't rule out your place on this earth because
you don't fit into the boxes drawn for you
Don't cry yourself to sleep because they don't
love you as you are

Find your truth and sing from your own hymn
sheet
Fall in love with humming your own song
Tap deep into the essence of your soul and find
comfort knowing that you have the sweet nectar
of your own truth to satisfy your own tongue
This world will shut you out
Let it
Don't knock on the doors begging to be let in
Stay where it feels safe, or adventure wherever
your curiosity leads
But find that place that unlocks new space
Space where you feel your heart can beat
uninterrupted
That you can free yourself and be worshipped in
your fullness
You were made to be whole
Don't break pieces off of you to satisfy someone
else's needs
You deserve every part of your beautiful body
Every word your voice wants to utter
You deserve to find safety in your very own
being
And be nurtured by another for exactly who you
choose to be
Loving yourself is about seeing the darkness
The flaws
And finding acceptance

Allowing yourself to be broken, or angry, or
jealous or scared
And giving yourself the time to heal through it
Recognise the places these emotions stem from
Releasing the trauma
You deserve to feel whole despite the broken
pieces
You are allowed to have holes
You are an angel of the divine.

20 Belonging - the roots of consciousness

Be longing
The longing to belong
Belonging to a cause, a passion, or someone
Putting our energy into more
Than the isolated self
Community & intimacy
Vital to our health
It is here that we become
So much more than we believe
Be longing to be one
With the earth and with the trees
It's not about ownership
It's the opposite in fact
That when you choose where you belong
Your power stays intact
Your soul begins to grow
Evolving in the spaces she feels safe
With the earth beneath our toes
And the sun shining on our face
The longing to belong
Finding sisters, brothers, kin
That recognise our oneness
That feel the love we hold within
An extension of the heart
We have carried from our birth

A return from spirit consciousness
To dance across the Earth
Deep within us we all know
There's a divine and sacred place
A womb that births new cycles
What we call the Human Race
But belonging can't be rushed
It happens when we're still
For us to centre
To grow roots
To soften into our own will
To trust that where we stand
Is exactly where we should be
Where we feel the deepest love
for a higher collective "WE".

21 You are She - let the light in

My love you blossom, you grow, you
overwhelm me with your beauty
Your smile is deep and pure and so full of love
I feel you soften and it moves me
Keep lowering those walls and moving
Shifting
Releasing
Growing

Soften more my darling and relax into how
peaceful this new space is
How much gentler life is
How open you are to receiving and what a
special gift you hold
Don't fight your emotions allow them to be and
feel them deeply
Don't be told your depths are too deep
You will not learn in the shallows
Hold space for yourself and fill that space with
love
Tell yourself daily how perfect you you are
How your flaws are your opportunities to learn
How your heartbreaks are opportunities to heal
Cry, be real, be true

Show your vulnerability and let it all fall out
Don't hold it in, enjoy the release
And accept a warm embrace to help you feel
safe
Let the light in. Let the love in
Don't be afraid
Face the fears knowing you are strong

You are beautiful
You are loved

You are SHE.

9 789358 738162